30 Minutes
... To Plan a Project

Trevor Young

**KOGAN
PAGE**

First published in 1997
Reprinted 1998

Kogan Page Limited
120 Pentonville Road
London N1 9JN

© Trevor Young, 1997

British Library Cataloguing in Publication Data

A CIP record for this book is available from the British Library.

ISBN 0 7494 2365 X

Typeset by Saxon Graphics Ltd, Derby
Printed and bound in Great Britain by Clays Ltd, St Ives plc

CONTENTS

The 30 Minutes Series

The *Kogan Page 30 Minutes Series* has been devised to give your confidence a boost when faced with tackling a new skill or challenge for the first time.

So the next time you're thrown in at the deep end and want to bring your skills up to scratch or pep up your career prospects, turn to the *30 Minutes Series* for help!

Titles available are:

30 Minutes Before Your Job Interview
30 Minutes Before a Meeting
30 Minutes Before a Presentation
30 Minutes to Boost Your Communication Skills
30 Minutes to Brainstorm Great Ideas
30 Minutes to Deal with Difficult People
30 Minutes to Succeed in Business Writing
30 Minutes to Master the Internet
30 Minutes to Make the Right Decision
30 Minutes to Make the Right Impression
30 Minutes to Plan a Project
30 Minutes to Prepare a Job Application
30 Minutes to Write a Business Plan
30 Minutes to Write a Marketing Plan
30 Minutes to Write a Report
30 Minutes to Write Sales Letters

Available from all good booksellers.
For further information on the series, please contact:

Kogan Page, 120 Pentonville Road, London N1 9JN
Tel: 0171 278 0433 Fax: 0171 837 6348

INTRODUCTION

Can you plan a project in thirty minutes? Even if it is small and does not involve anyone else you need more time. Planning is about organizing the future – or at least the short term future, then ensuring everyone involved understands their role and what they must do for success. Planning is a convenient way to communicate the organization of the short term future showing what must be done, who must do it (the work), when and where it must be done and the deadlines or time targets that must be met.

What do you need from this book? Your personal expectations are unknown to me and I have no way of exploring them to ensure the contents are just right for you. Faced with this inevitable constraint I have attempted to give you a book that:

- is easy to read

- gives you a short briefing of essential principles

- provides you with seven simple steps to follow

- will enable you to confidently plan your next project more effectively.

We are surrounded at work today by experts at everything and this is particularly true when planning is mentioned. Have you noticed that everyone claims to be a good planner? When you have read this book you can find out who does know how to plan a project effectively and seek to learn more from them and their experiences. Take every opportunity to obtain coaching and guidance from such an expert. Their practical knowledge is an invaluable asset that is often under-rated by their colleagues and the organization.

The planning process is designed for use with your project team. There are frequent opportunities for small, single person projects and the techniques described here are still valid and will help you achieve success. If you are the 'team' take every opportunity to seek guidance from experienced colleagues when you are not sure of the work content. Attempt to derive your workload carefully and stick to the plan.

It is easy to be tyrannised by urgency and dive straight in to start work without any planning. It is clearly visible that something is happening! But are the right things being done? Are they in the right order? You can never be sure until you discover what has not been done or what assumptions have been made – in error!

Then you are faced with rework which takes up much time and effort.

Think of planning as an investment to save time later.

The process steps described here are based on practical experience. My intention is to provide a short briefing to enable you to plan the next project effectively and achieve a successful outcome. The process is a relatively simple one but it is never easy and does need a strong commitment, determination and desire for success. Planning is hard work, fun, frustrating, more fun and more hard work but seeing it eventually working is very rewarding and a huge learning experience every time. I wish you success with all your efforts in future.

Trevor L Young
July 1997

THE PLANNING PROCESS

Project planning is a logical process to ensure the work of your project can be carried out: in an organized and structured manner; reducing risks and uncertainty to a minimum; establishing clear standards of quality and performance; securing the results in the minimum time and cost.

Planning is a dynamic process, always subject to revision and improvement as the project work proceeds. Problems arising must be promptly resolved and actions taken to maintain agreed targets and deadlines. Planning only really stops when you reach the day you can confidently shout 'complete' and you have a delighted customer.

Who needs to be involved?

A project plan is a collection of ideas and knowledge that has been organized into packages of work. Do you have all the necessary knowledge, infinite ideas and wide experience? Will you do all the work with no-one else involved at any stage of the project? Such a project is unusual! In practice your skill must lie in getting the ideas and knowledge from as many people as possible. This does not mean you must consult the whole organization. It is potentially dangerous for the project to ignore real skills of others who can make a significant contribution to success.

If six people planned the same project independently, the results would show extensive variation. Put the six people together and derive a plan by consensus where all agree it is right, the result must have a higher chance of success. Planning is a team activity, so apart from yourself invite the project team (if you have one) and others with relevant skills to get involved in your planning session. If you do not have a team still invite others to get involved, their experience can save you much time later. The benefit of teamwork in project planning is clarity of purpose, understanding and acceptance by everyone. This creates commitment and a desire to win – a successful project. Remember, no one wants to be associated with failure.

The process

The project planning process we will use is derived as seven steps or blocks of activity:

- review the project definition

- derive the project logic

- prepare the initial schedule

- resource and cost analysis

- optimize and meet customer needs

- validation and plan approval
- launch the project.

The jargon

Project planning uses a collection of terms which may be unfamiliar. The common ones we will use here are given below:

- *task* – a piece of work carried out by one person
- *activity* – a package of work comprising several tasks, carried out by one or more people
- *key stage* – a special activity that is often a group of activities
- *dependency* – the logical link between activities, where every one of the inputs to an activity are directly dependent on the outputs of another
- *logic diagram* – the graphic display of all the key stages of the project showing their dependency links
- *resource* – the individual person with responsibility to ensure some work is completed on time
- *work breakdown structure* – a graphic display of all the work of the project, showing the task lists for each key stage
- *sponsor* – the individual to whom you report as project leader – usually a senior manager who is accountable for the project success
- *stakeholder* – any individual who has an interest in the project results: the customer, other managers, finance department, contractors, suppliers, end users, etc.

Others will be defined as we proceed through the process.

STEP 1

REVIEW THE PROJECT DEFINITION

It is always necessary to validate the project definition before you start planning what has to be done. The process of definition should have clearly established why the project is necessary now and what outcomes are expected. Everyone involved in planning must understand this definition before they can realistically contribute to deriving a project plan. The essential elements of definition should have included:

A statement of need or opportunity

This is a concise statement of why the project is required at the current time, possibly to address a particular problem or take advantage of an opportunity presented to the organization. This is the rationale for the project and provides the essential background to why the project is being established.

A statement of the project overall objective

It is convenient for communicating to everyone what your project is aiming to achieve in a general sense, usually with the timescale or deadlines for completion stated. Such statements are preferably concise and convey clarity of purpose.

The objective is to derive, by January 1998, a new marketing strategy with integrated implementation plans for the operating divisions for the period 1998 – 2000.

A list of the constraints and assumptions

When a project starts it is frequently necessary to make some assumptions, possibly about money, available people, technology required, skills required, space or equipment needs etc. Assumptions have a habit of being easily forgotten as the project proceeds until a problem occurs. Then someone remembers what was assumed at the outset – incorrectly! All assumptions must be recorded as they often become issues later that must be resolved. Similarly few projects have the luxury of no constraints. There are always some restrictions on the project all the way to the completion point and these are usually associated with:

- people – the *resources* and their skills to do the work.

- money – the capital and revenue available.

- time – the results have a deadline for you to achieve.

You may have been given a *Business Critical Date* when the results must be available and any slippage is critical to forecast business performance.

A list of deliverables and benefits

In your earlier discussions with the project stakeholders you will have identified their needs and what they expect to get from your future efforts. Meeting stakeholder expectations is never easy as the hidden agendas are not always exposed at the outset. Your purpose is to ensure you have understood their needs and offered what you believe are a set of project requirements that meet these needs and as many expectations as reasonably possible in the time desired.

These requirements are stated as the:

- *deliverables* – the tangible and measurable results to be achieved, both interim and at completion point.

- *benefits* – the measurable subsequent benefits to the customer or your organization, usually measured in financial terms as a yield against time, eg. income, contribution or cost savings.

Deliverables and benefits should meet the SMART test:

- **S**pecific – clearly described and defined

- **M**easurable – clearly defined means of measuring the achievement with metrics

- **A**chievable – with the skills available in the current environment

- **R**ealistic – attainable with current knowledge and not presenting huge risks and unknowns

- **T**imebound – limited by a completion date based on real and known needs.

A project budget

The cost of the project may be established early during the definition phase. It may be based on previous similar projects or it may be inspired guesswork! Costs are usually divided into capital and revenue costs. The former is subject to organization policy and procedures that may take some time to complete. Revenue costs are often ignored and absorbed as part of general operating costs. For good project control resource costs should be measured as this allows a more comprehensive cost/benefit analysis to be completed. Without this data the real cost of the project is hidden so the return on the investment of people's time is never accurately exposed. The real budget can only be accurately established after the plans are derived and fully costed.

An analysis of the risks

All projects carry risks as a burdensome baggage! You cannot afford to ignore them as every unexpected problem that arises during the project work has come from an unidentified risk – that you should have anticipated. Risks can be divided into three types:

- business risk – impacts on current business activity or future performance

- project – associated with the 'technical' part of the project, ie. technology, equipment performance etc.

- process – associated with the processes and procedures you employ to complete the project on time.

You should have examined each with your team and identified any high risks – those with a serious impact and have a high probability of occurrence. Such risks must be subject to contingent action plans or even preventative actions now, before you start planning. Keep a record of such risks for continuous review and updating. Remind the project team regularly to anticipate these and new risks.

13

The project strategy and skills required

A strategy for the project should now exist. Are you following more than one option to achieve your objective? Do you need different skill-sets in your resources for these options?

Ensure you and your team understand the strategy agreed and consider it is still a valid approach. Validate any earlier decisions to use sub-contractors for part of the work or reuse existing equipment or technology. Confirm any new or specialized skills needed for the project that do not currently exist in the organization and what actions must be taken to correct this situation.

Review the definition documentation

With your sponsor and team together, review all these elements and the recorded information. Confirm everyone understands this definition – it is the foundation of planning. A weak foundation will lead to poor planning and significantly reduce your chances of achieving a successful result. If there are doubts or concerns about any aspect of the definition, then you must return to clarify and validate these parts again with the key stakeholders. This does not mean you cannot change anything later, it just ensures that subsequent changes to the project requirements can be examined in a controlled manner. It is essential for you to ensure that everyone is starting from the same position (ie. clarity of understanding and consensus agreement) when planning starts!

STEP 2

DERIVE THE PROJECT LOGIC

Few projects enjoy the luxury of progressing to completion without changes to the definition. People have the habit of changing their minds through:

- creativity – generating new ideas

- recollection – bringing forgotten data into the picture

- the environment – the situation in the organization changes

- the market – the external influences change with time.

Since your efforts are spread over a defined period of time, the project is vulnerable to all of these influences. You must display a flexible approach to accommodate these variations. This does not mean all amendments will be feasible or acceptable, but you cannot ignore requests to change something. Each must be examined relative to achieving success and satisfying your customer and other stakeholders.

Planning is therefore a continuous process throughout the project life and only finishes when all the results are handed over to the customer and accepted.

The planning meeting

Set up your first planning meeting to give everyone adequate time to think about their contributions. Decide who you need present apart from your core team. Check that everyone is available and can attend, informing them about:

- the purpose of the meeting
- the start time and expected finish time
- the outputs you expect to achieve.

Ask attendees to give some thought to what they expect will need to be done in the project. Ask your sponsor to attend and open the meeting, focusing particularly on:

- reasons for the project
- why it is important now
- priority relative to other work and projects
- context in the current business plan and strategy
- concern for success
- the benefits.

After the introduction, you can review the primary objectives, particularly for the benefit of those extra people you have invited to join the planning meeting. List out the main deliverables on a flip chart and keep this on view to remind everyone.

Start the planning process by brainstorming the activities to be carried out. Ask the question:

What do we have to do to achieve these results?

Remind everyone of the rules of brainstorming:

- appoint a scribe
- one at a time please
- suspend all judgement – no critical remarks
- ban all discussion or debate
- write everything down on the flip chart – even duplicates.

The objective is to achieve quantity not quality at this stage. As each sheet of flip chart fills with activities, paper the walls of the meeting room with paper! Do not concern yourself with:

- *time* – how long each activity will take to complete
- *resource* – who is going to do the work
- *politics* – whether something is allowed or not.

After 1–2 hours you will have a formidable list of activities, some of which may be irrelevant. When the team seems to reach 'dry-out' point, stop the brainstorming and allow everyone to review the lists produced. Add or remove activities as new ideas and thoughts appear.

At this stage it is often difficult to see how you can organize a long list of activities and prioritize them for the plan. To help this process it is necessary to reduce the list and we can do this by clustering. The objective is to group related tasks together to form a cluster. This is often based on functions or departments involved. Aim to reduce your list to 100 or fewer, but preferably not fewer than 30. This reduced list is now the key stages of the project. Because you have reduced the list to manageable proportions it becomes easier to prioritize the activities.

The taskboarding process

This employs the essential principle of *dependency* to determine the order or sequence of the work. This is based on asking questions:

> *What must we do first?*

> *What can we now do using the outputs of the first activities?*

We continue this process, asking what we can do using the outputs of one activity as inputs to the next one or more activities. Eventually all the activities will be used up to give us the *project logic*.

1. A convenient and powerful way to carry out this process is to write each key stage activity on a post-it note and develop the logic as a diagram on the meeting room wall: Set up a large sheet of paper on the wall (use flip chart sheets or wallpaper lining paper).

2. Mark the left-hand side with a large 'S' for the project start and mark the right-hand side with a large 'F' for the project finish.

3. Position the post-it notes with the initial key stages next

to the start point. Then asking the above questions, identify the next key stages using the outputs from the initial post-it notes. Position these to the right of the first set.

4. Then continue the process, positioning the post-it notes in the logical order of the work, moving across the paper from left to right towards the finish point.

5. Continue until all the post-it notes have been used and you reach the finish point.

6. With your team review the logic and question the position of each post-it note in the sequencing.

7. When you are satisfied that everyone agrees the logic connect the post-it notes together with arrows to show the flow and dependency link (always use a pencil!).

8. CHECK that each post-it note has an arrow entering the left-hand side as an input and an arrow exiting from the right-hand side as an output.

9. VALIDATE the logic by working backwards from the finish, asking *'What must be done last?'* and then *'What must be done before this?'* repeatedly until you reach the start point.

You have now derived the project *logic diagram* which is the foundation of your plan. This diagram represents all the work that must be done. As it is derived by compressing many tasks into each key stage, forgotten tasks are hidden at present. The accuracy is therefore improved by this compression process, although it may still be necessary to expand the diagram by splitting or adding additional key stages.

The Work Breakdown Structure (WBS)

The logic diagram forms the top level of a hierarchical breakdown of all the work of the project as shown below. This diagram does not normally include dependency links. Each key stage at Level 1 can be expanded to show the list of included activities and tasks at the lower levels. Depending on the size of the project you can break down the project to expose all the detail and task lists at each level or *layer* of the plan.

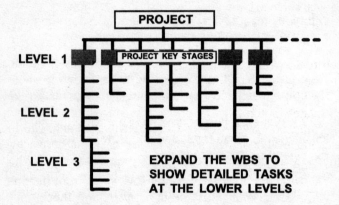

You can go further and use the taskboarding concept to derive the logic diagram for all the tasks inside any key stage. Eventually you can use the WBS to allocate responsibilities for the individual tasks, add in planned completion dates, then use the lists for monitoring progress.

Other useful methods

When you are working with a team, brainstorming together is a valuable way of utilizing team experience and skills to identify activities. If you are working alone on a project other methods are available. You can use some problem-solving tools and structured brainstorming tools like mind maps and what-what diagrams. All will help you to derive a list of activities from which the key stages are developed.

The what-what diagram

This technique is often useful for second and third level planning of the WBS. Take a large sheet of paper and the centre of the left-hand side write out one or more deliverables, enclosed in a box. Then ask the question:

What do I have to do to achieve this?

Write down the activities you decide are required as a list to the right of the initial box.

When you think you have identified all the initial key activities (potentially the project key stages) repeat the initial question over each of these activities to generate the second level of activities to be carried out. Add these activities to your diagram. If appropriate you can ask the 'What' question three or more times to generate even more detail. Three times is frequently sufficient to find the detail down to task level.

This is effectively your WBS without the dependencies and the data generated can then be used to derive the logic diagram.

If you have generated an activity list with the team and then derived the key stages of your project, you can encourage your team to use this technique to develop the detail of each key stage.

Facing problems?

The 'what–what' diagram can be used very effectively for

problem solving. Replace the deliverable in the box with the effects we perceive because of the problem and instead of asking 'What' we ask:

Why does this happen?

Now write the primary list of why it happens – the causes, to the right of the box as before and repeat the question over each primary cause identified. The process of asking 'Why' can be repeated as often as appropriate to generate a list of causes and sub-causes. Then by a process of eliminating the most unlikely causes you will be left with a list of the *most likely causes* of the problem. You can then start to seek a solution more effectively by finding ways to eradicate the causes you have identified.

A word about templates

It is valuable and time-saving to generate templates for some projects. A template is a generic plan for similar projects such as new product development, that is used over and over.

Your project logic can become such a template once it has been thoroughly tested and proved to be accurate with a high probability of success. It is preferable to keep templates without resource and time data as this may vary from project to project. Keep your estimating records and past data separately.

> **CAUTION: A template only saves time if it is carefully validated each time before use to ensure nothing is missing or to identify some activities that are not required.**

STEP 3

PREPARE THE PROJECT SCHEDULE

A schedule is a plan with all the dates for the work fixed and accepted by the customer. The schedule is based on our logic diagram with real time and resources – the people to do the work, identified and committed. It will also be the basis of the final budget for the project to enable accurate cost control. To derive the schedule we need to follow some essential process steps:

Handing out responsibilities

When the team has agreed the logic diagram is correct (based on current information) you can allocate individual responsibilities. Each key stage must have an 'owner' who is responsible for ensuring the work gets done – either by themselves or with others.

When you allocate responsibility take care to ensure the individual selected:

■ has appropriate skills, experience and knowledge

- has enough time to do the work
- has the support and commitment of their line manager
- is familiar with the use of planning techniques
- understands what is expected
- accepts the responsibility

This usually means each team member will be responsible for more than one key stage.

> *Record all allocated responsibilities and inform the team and stakeholders. Always keep this record up to date.*

Then ask each key stage owner to:

- identify all the tasks inside their key stage(s)
- derive time estimates for every task to find the time each key stage will take to complete – the *duration*.

Look inside the key stages

Some of the detail of tasks inside each key stage will have been identified during the initial brainstorming. This list must now be reviewed and validated by an expert, adding more tasks if appropriate or removing any not required. Tasks forgotten earlier can be identified along with specific tasks needed to avoid or minimize risks occurring. Encourage the key stage owners to try and assemble the list into the right sequence by creating a logic diagram for each key stage.

This generates a collection of small logic diagrams like a family derived from the key stage logic diagram at the top level.

How long do the key stages take?

The key stage owners must then use their expertise to generate realistic estimates of working time for each task to arrive at a total time for each key stage – the *duration*.

> *Ensure everyone uses the same units and standards when estimating durations.*

The perfect plan is elusive because we do not know what it actually looks like, as there are always risks and unknowns that can affect our intentions. There are many reasons why plans go wrong:

- poor understanding of the project requirements
- missing activities and tasks identified later
- changes resulting from modified objectives
- over-optimistic estimates
- assumptions not checked and validated
- issues not resolved – still awaiting management decisions
- poor estimating
- missing skills and low confidence levels
- complexity or difficulty of the work not understood

All have an impact on estimates of time to do the work and these estimates are frequently blamed for subsequent failure. The overall time is always the most vulnerable aspect of any project because it is the first thing to suffer when something goes wrong. Perhaps this is due to insufficient effort given to getting the estimates in the first place and then subjecting them to continual review and validation.

A closer look at estimating

Estimates come from three sources:

1. *Recorded historical data* – the archive of past projects from which data is analysed, trends identified and standards or norms established for different types of work.

2. *Past experience* – you and your key stage owners have heaps of experience on previous projects. Can you remember the details or find them now?

3. *The 'expert'* – a consultant or well established and proven standards to give accurate data.

It is common for 1. not to exist, at least formally, although you may have some past project files for reference. Project files today are often electronic, not hard copy, so access to data some time after the event may not be easy. Is 3. possible? If your project involves creative work there are no real experts although you may be surrounded by plenty of amateurs!

So you are left with the experience and judgement of yourself and the key stage owners. Encourage them to:

- talk to others about the time to complete tasks to derive estimates from a range of opinion

- be realistic about time particularly for complex work

- avoid adding contingencies as a 'safety margin'

- clearly identify tasks needing more than one person

- provisionally decide how many people are to be required for the 'multiple-resourced' tasks (this has to be provisional as you cannot be sure they are available yet).

NOTE: Contingencies are for the unexpected and forgotten tasks – NOT a safety margin to cover poor estimating of the known tasks!

A decision to identify a task as multiple-resourced is based on necessity for the type of work NOT just to save time. Adding more resource to a task does not guarantee the time is reduced by 50 per cent.

So who or what goes wrong?

Everyone does. Some people don't want to work in your project – and tell you so emphatically. Others will jump at the chance and immediately say, 'Yes, great.' In truth though do you know if they really have enough time to do the work? The issue that can lead to so much conflict in project work is the *capacity problem*. Of course if you have a dedicated team for your project this is not such a problem. All the team's available time – their capacity to do the work – is available to you.

Watch out for arsonists!

They are always about, lighting the fires of crisis and then demanding the temporary return of one or more of your team to 'solve this urgent problem. It will only take a morning!' And two days later your team is still not back to project work!

Yes, problems in keeping the business moving are always likely to happen and your team is an obvious source of available people for troubleshooting and instant problem solving. So be prepared to lose some capacity in the team. It will happen and this is particularly frustrating during the planning phase of a project. You are trying to keep the team together at all times to ensure concensus agreement, acceptance, commitment and create good

27

teamworking. We are often tyrannized by urgency at the expense of importance. Try to keep everyone focused on the project and involve the sponsor regularly – remember this person wants the results and should give you support!

The capacity problem

Capacity – the time each of us has available every day for project work. If you have a team who are part-time and committed to other activities such as day-to-day operations to keep the business moving, capacity issues often lead to conflict. Project work is an additional burden that many have no capacity to include.

Ask yourself what you do in a day (or week). Does it break down to:

1. Operational work – associated with keeping the business moving, dealing with customer issues, continuous improvement, sustaining the organization's fitness.

2. Fire-fighting – reacting to 'urgent' problems in production, service functions or customer requirements often at the expense of the really important.

3. Anything else – involvement in the project

Does this pattern show a real capacity for project work? You must question anyone with little capacity for the work accepting the responsibility. People may be keen to work with you and say 'Yes' to your invitation, but a low capacity (less than 10 per cent) is likely to be subject to considerable interruption since project work is given a low priority.

Success in project work is dependent on you ensuring everyone has a reasonable capacity consistent with the time needed to maintain quality and performance.

Frequently the project work is temporarily suspended

with a comment: 'You can make up the time later!' How this is achieved is never disclosed as the higher stress level, once reached, never seems to reduce to manageable proportions again. The consequences may be serious for the work and health!

This leads to frustration, demotivation, lower quality, loss of attention to detail, and frequently much rework to correct errors or 'sloppy' work. It also leads to 'back tracking' or going over previous work done. This is due to the work being broken down into small chunks with large time slices in between. It is necessary to remember what was done last time before starting the next chunk – and then new ideas lead to changes, rework and use up valuable time.

What can you do?

Check out the capacity situation for everyone assigned responsibilities in the project. If the pattern is showing 10 per cent or less ask if this is really sufficient for your needs.

Try to:

- persuade team members and their managers that a high capacity, particularly at peak loading periods in the project is more effective

- ensure the team is relieved of some operational duties to create capacity

- seek commitments from the line managers that team members will not be called back for reactive situations by stressing the importance and strategic context of your project.

Give particular attention to discovering the other work commitments of the team members. Rather than admit lack of time, some people will give over-optimistic estimates and then be faced with a 'forced fit'. Remember an estimate is an opinion if it is not backed up with real data.

> *Review and validate estimates throughout the project with current available information*

Look out for time robbers!

Time is one of our most valuable commodities and its value is well recognized by others. The consequence of the many ways we lose time is a reduction in productive output. These time robbers can reduce the effective week to less than four working days. Frequent robbers of time include:

- meetings we don't want to attend
- reacting to 'urgent' problems and situations
- reading journals and other media
- e-mail you are not directly affected by
- chasing information
- looking for lost data
- interruptions by others
- wanderlust – impulsive desire to interrupt others for a chat!

You can do little to avoid them sometimes but do alert your team they must in future keep a clear focus on the project work and the durations agreed in the plan.

> *Keep a record of all estimates of the project activities and update any changes that occur. Note the actual durations for future reference.*

How long will the project take?

When you are satisfied you have acceptable estimates, write the duration for each key stage on the post-it notes. Now you can find the total project time. The logic diagram gives you a number of alternative ways to get from the start to the finish just like a road map. Begin at the start and trace each available pathway through to the finish, adding the durations as you pass through each post-it note on the path.

Record the total duration for each path and check that you follow every available route to the finish. The highest number represents the longest route and this is the *minimum total project time* with your current estimates. This is also known as the *critical path* of the project. The critical path is always the *longest* path prevailing at any time and must be monitored closely. Any extension of the critical path will extend the project beyond the original finish date.

The critical path is not fixed since it is based on the assumption that all durations are real and never modified. When you come to do the work some key stages may take more time and some less time than estimated. The consequence is a change to the critical path. This dynamic quality is important to understand and monitor carefully. Parts of the project you thought were non-critical can suddenly become critical due to slippages occurring.

A closer understanding of the situation at any time is available to you through *critical path analysis*. If you decide this rigorous analysis is not necessary then the time information can be displayed in a simple bar chart.

Displaying time data in chart form

The widely accepted method of displaying time information graphically for projects is the simple *bar chart*. An example is shown overleaf.

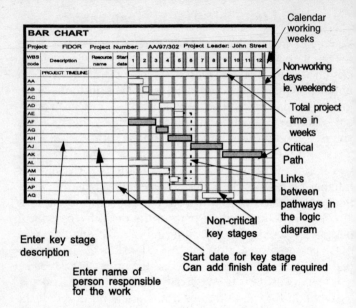

Enter key stage description

Enter name of person responsible for the work

Start date for key stage
Can add finish date if required

Duration time for each key stage or task is represented by a rectangular bar or box, with the length measured against a horizontal time line. Each pathway is marked on the chart from the first key stage in the pathway at project start date.

The links (merges) of the different pathways can be shown with broken lines and the dependency links drawn in with arrows if required. The critical path is often highlighted in a different colour. You can also add additional data on the chart if it helps everyone involved in the work, eg dates for progress meetings. This type of chart is regularly updated during the progress of the work by shading in the bar to show the percentage complete of all the currently active key stages. The scale is drawn to suit the total project timescale and can be in hours, days, working weeks or even months.

Analysing the logic diagram

The process of analysis is based on two essential properties of the logic diagram:

- The longest path (ie highest total duration) is critical and none of the key stages on this path can be extended without extending the total project time

- All other key stages not on the critical path have some spare time associated with them – known as the *total float*.

The purpose of analysis is to determine the spare time. If a key stage has spare time it can start at any point within a defined range of dates – without extending the project. Knowledge of this information is valuable to help you take decisions about utilizing windows of opportunity for available resources, equipment, access to systems, testing etc.

The analysis involves summing durations between the start and finish to determine the earliest start and finish times. The earliest finish time of the last key stage is the total project time. This is the *forward pass* calculation.

The process is then repeated in reverse, working from the finish, subtracting durations at each key stage, to determine the latest finish and start times.

When you reach the start post-it, one of the first key stages will show a late start of zero time. This is the *backward pass* calculation.

If your calculations do not return to a zero in one of the initial key stages you have made an arithmetic error! Two essential rules must be followed:

1. In the forward pass:

> When two or more key stages merge into another, take the HIGHEST of the *earliest finish times* as the *earliest start time* of the next key stage.

2. In the backward pass:

> At the same type of merge situation, take the LOWEST of the *latest start times* for the *latest finish time* in the preceding key stage.

The calculation of the spare time or total float for each key stage is then made by taking the arithmetic difference between:

- the *earliest start time* and the *latest start time*
- the *earliest finish time* and the *latest finish time*.

Both will give you the same result and the figure obtained is the total float for the key stage.

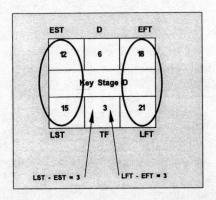

Critical key stages and activities by definition, have ZERO TOTAL FLOAT – no spare time!

Finally you can enter the data into a bar chart or as it is more commonly known the *Gantt Chart* (after Henry Gantt). The difference in this chart is the display of the amount of total float in the non-critical key stages. This gives you the freedom to take decisions about starting some work late without affecting the total project time. This may be due to resource availability or other fixed windows such as equipment availability.

The bars representing the key stages are initially always drawn starting at the earliest start time. This enables you to take decisions about the use of float later. Point out to everyone involved that they should not take arbitrary decisions to start some work late because there is float time available.

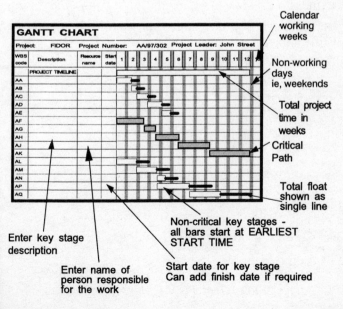

35

Total float time should only be utilised with your consent as project leader. You may need this spare time later for problem solving.

STEP 4

RESOURCE AND COST ANALYSIS

Now that you have a schedule that seems to be acceptable to the sponsor you need to provide resources to do the work. Some of the estimates your key stage owners have derived may be based on one or more people being involved. Now you need to clarify this situation with a more detailed analysis of people needed to do the work. The subsidiary steps are shown below.

Confirm the detail inside the key stages

Before the analysis can start you must ask your key stage owners to confirm they have opened up their key stages to expose the details of the task lists in each. Encourage them to use the taskboarding technique to find the dependencies and locate the critical path through the key stage. Although this may not be part of the project critical path it will help you locate the shortest time to complete any key stage. You are now completing the Work Breakdown Structure for your project.

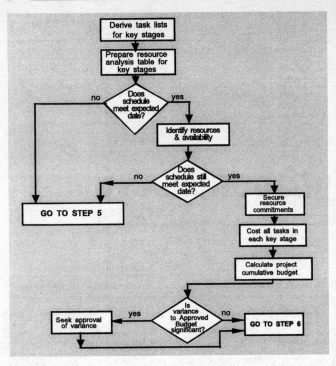

Create a table of resource needs

Make up a table of the resources needed for the tasks inside each key stage, based on skill type. Later you can assign tasks to individuals by name as shown below. This table will identify what resources you are going to need for each key stage.

Review the estimates and confirm that the number of resources of each type are correct. Add or remove additional resources as you consider necessary. At this stage you are assessing the ideal requirements and you do not

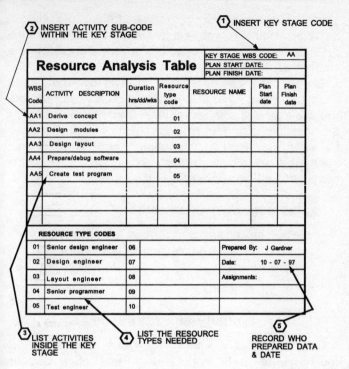

② INSERT ACTIVITY SUB-CODE WITHIN THE KEY STAGE

① INSERT KEY STAGE CODE

Resource Analysis Table

KEY STAGE WBS CODE: AA
PLAN START DATE:
PLAN FINISH DATE:

WBS Code	ACTIVITY DESCRIPTION	Duration hrs/dd/wks	Resource type code	RESOURCE NAME	Plan Start date	Plan Finish date
AA1	Derive concept		01			
AA2	Design modules		02			
AA3	Design layout		03			
AA4	Prepare/debug software		04			
AA5	Create test program		05			

RESOURCE TYPE CODES

01	Senior design engineer	06		
02	Design engineer	07		Prepared By: J Gardner
03	Layout engineer	08		Date: 10 - 07 - 97
04	Senior programmer	09		Assignments:
05	Test engineer	10		

③ LIST ACTIVITIES INSIDE THE KEY STAGE

④ LIST THE RESOURCE TYPES NEEDED

⑤ RECORD WHO PREPARED DATA & DATE

know if these people can be available for the work when the schedule dictates specific dates.

A planning dilemma – or nightmare!

The work so far has given you:

- a schedule with a completion date

- an analysis of the resources required by skill type only.

You have not identified the actual people who will be

39

allocated the work at the appropriate time. Is the schedule really acceptable to your customer? You must have some preliminary discussions with the sponsor and customer to clarify their current position.

Is there any possibility that you will be faced with a change of mind – has the original *expected date* (the customer's expected completion date) mysteriously shifted? If the schedule is no longer acceptable you must find a way to meet the revised expectation. There is little point attempting to secure resource commitments from line managers until you have revised the schedule.

SCHEDULE NOT ACCEPTABLE?

Before proceeding any further with identifying and securing resources you must optimize the schedule.

JUMP NOW TO STEP 5

Identify the resources

If the schedule is acceptable you can proceed to identify the people to do the work. This is a team effort, deciding who you would like to have assigned to the project. As much of the work will be carried out in addition to continuing business responsibilities, you cannot make these assignments without consulting the respective line managers. You are now faced with a re-iterative process of:

- identifying the resources needed;

- consulting each person about their current and forecast future loading and capacity;

- consulting the line manager to seek a commitment for release to work on the project for the periods identified.

40

It is important to ensure the line managers understand the importance and strategic context of your project. The line managers may consider they cannot spare their people who are already heavily loaded. They may feel negative about the project and not want to help you. If necessary resort to getting additional support from your sponsor.

It would be an amazing coincidence if all the resources you need are offered and made available without any difficulties. In practice your schedule will expand and compress as you locate the right people and secure commitments from the line managers. With one eye on the estimates you must find enough resources to maintain the schedule. Sometimes you will find no resource available and you must consider:

- taking on contract staff

- sub-contracting part of the work

- asking team members to find more capacity

- extending the schedule to allow for periods of availability and non-availability.

If the schedule is extended you must try to compress it again by applying additional resources if you can locate them. Alternatively apply the techniques discussed in Step 5. Remember that just adding more resources does not always reduce durations by the same factor – doubling resources does not always reduce duration by 50 per cent – communication and co-ordination take up some of the time. A 30 per cent reduction is a safer assumption unless you can clearly divide the work into sensible chunks between more than one person.

Eventually you will reach a point where you have promises of resources to do the work and you have the best schedule you can achieve in the current circumstances. Then ask:

Is this schedule still acceptable to the customer?

If the response is negative then you have two options:

- persuade the customer that the schedule you are now proposing is based on a full analysis and the best you can hope for in the current business climate

- alert your sponsor to the issue and working together seek ways to find additional resources to do the work.

Although the second option may yield some benefit you are much more likely to need your negotiating skills to arrive at a satisfactory conclusion in dialogue with your customer. You must also review the project risks before finalizing the schedule as your conversations should include an examination of the areas of the project subject to high risk. (See Step 6). If the response is positive update the resource analysis tables to show:

- the name of each person assigned to the tasks

- the name of the line manager for each assignment

- the dates the work must be started and completed.

Issue these tables to the line managers as a record of the commitments they have made with you. Persuade them to sign the records as a signal of acceptance. Do not rely on all these commitments being met without difficulty. The business environment is continually changing and you must take this into account.

Regularly review the resource needs and commitments needed to maintain the schedule dates.

Work out the project costs

Are you required to work with a budget and control the costs? Have you been given an initial budget?

It is only as the Work Breakdown Structure is fully developed that you can derive the real costs of the planned work. Taking each key stage in turn, assess the costs of all the tasks and sum these to provide a key stage cost. With all the key stages costed you can plot a simple cumulative cost for the project against time. This can be used for cost control and deriving a cash flow forecast if required.

The costs derived in this way are often regarded as the *operating budget* because it is based on real data. Any earlier budget is termed the *approved budget* or *primary budget* based on initial estimates – often a mixture of inspired guesswork and previous experience!

> *A significant negative variance of the operating budget (ie higher cost) is an issue that must be resolved with the sponsor and customer NOW.*

What are the inputs to the operating budget?

Input data for deriving a budget have a number of common elements. Budgeting processes and controls vary for different organizations, so consult your finance department for policy guidelines.

Typical costs in the budget include:

- resource costs – either a global rate or by grade
- revenue costs to run the project 'office'
- other consumed or converted materials
- overhead costs – rent, rates, air conditioning, lighting, etc.

- depreciated purchases, eg computers, printers, etc.

- capital costs – hardware, equipment, etc.

- sub-contract costs

Line managers are normally concerned primarily with cost centre finances and the amount of under- or overspend. Project costs are given a lower level of importance – the people are employed anyway! But you cannot demonstrate the value of a project based on cost versus benefit yielded unless a financial plan is prepared and agreed and this is given a separate cost centre.

A financial plan

This will tell you and your team:

- the costs for each key stage

- who is accountable for these costs

- authorizations and limits of authority

- a cash flow forecast

- a schedule of commitments made

- the benefits to be yielded by the project.

Since costs are usually more visible to management than day-to-day progress, it is preferable to maintain your own records of costs incurred and commitments made.

This is essential where the finance department only record costs based on invoicing, not purchasing. The commitment made weeks or months earlier is not adjusted against the budget which then looks remarkably healthy. Set up some simple tables or use a spreadsheet to record all costs incurred as they happen. You will know exactly the status of your project budget.

The Work Breakdown Structure must be kept up to date to reflect any changes that occur in the plan. The breakdown of work is the basis of any forecasting you are asked to provide for cash flow or future costs to complete the project.

Prepare to regularly compare the reported project costs with your own records. Resolve any variances and clarify the true state of the budget.

Are contingencies necessary?

Contingency funds are presumed necessary to cover the unknown – forgotten costs or specific costs with doubtful accuracy. It is not a 'pot of gold' for you to take a handful when cost overruns occur due to poor estimating! To be accurate contingency is normally seen as a greater need for areas of the project with higher risk. So the amount available varies with project time rather than a global percentage based on total project cost. Using this principle, you can estimate the greater need for contingency funds after you have reviewed the project risks in Step 6. Then you can finalize the operating budget and request approval.

STEP 5

OPTIMIZE TO MEET CUSTOMER NEEDS

Now that you have analysed your initial schedule for resource needs you must check the results to ensure you can meet the customer's expectations. This is yet another reiterative process starting with asking some fundamental questions?

1. Is the initial definition still valid – has anything changed?

2. Does the plan reflect all definition changes?

3. Have you taken account of risks identified earlier?

4. Does the plan finish date meet customer needs?

5. Has the plan resource and cost analysis been derived?

The subsidiary steps of optimization are shown below.

Changes to the definition

If the initial definition has been modified during the planning

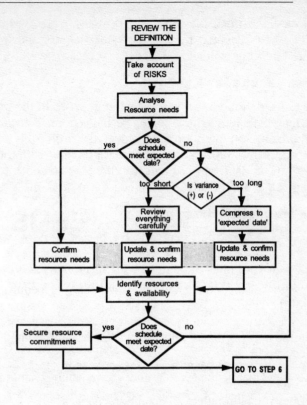

process then you must update the definition documents and submit them for further approval and acceptance with the plans. Perhaps the changes are due to:

- customer change of mind

- sponsor change of mind

- difficulties exposed during planning

- changes to the business situation.

You cannot launch the project work until all changes are ratified and accepted by your key stakeholders and fully written into the plan and schedule.

What about the risks?

The risks identified during the definition phase of the project may have highlighted some specific actions to include in the plan. The intention is to reduce the probability of a risk occurring and limit the impact if possible. You know where these risks will take effect in the plan so check that all agreed action plans are included.

The completion date

If your customer has given you an *expected date* for completion, does your initial schedule meet this requirement? If all your estimates are agreed as realistic then the result is your best shot! It is a rare event if it really is acceptable without some optimization.

> *Although it is not always a legal and binding document the plan is a form of contract, which once accepted, you have to do everything necessary to maintain.*

Schedule too short!

Yes, if you are very, very lucky. Don't get too excited yet because something may be wrong. Exercise caution and review everything:

- Are all deliverables clearly defined in the plan?
- Have any key stages been missed?
- Have any tasks inside the key stages been missed?

- Have you taken account of all quality requirements?

- How over-optimistic are the key stage estimates?

- Have you taken account of holidays and non-working days?

- Have you allowed for all the known high risks?

- Have you taken account of technical complexity?

- How accurate is your resource analysis?

- Do all the skills needed exist now?

If the review does not expose any errors then you can truly celebrate. Before telling your customer you have to secure all the resource commitments from line managers. This could easily upset everything if you discover a serious shortage of available people. Consider adding a 'cushion' of some extra time for security – perhaps 5 per cent to give you some room to manoeuvre in negotiating.

Schedule too long!

How often does this happen? It may be the customer and the sponsor have not understood the amount of detailed work involved. If you can convince them that you have considered all the factors listed in the previous section, you may succeed in getting the schedule accepted as it stands.

You must balance the length of the project with the business need to seek an optimum that:

- satisfies or better still delights the customer

- ensures a high quality standard

- can realistically be completed with available resources

- meets the needs of the business in generating benefits at the desired time.

Meeting these four criteria is easier said than practically achievable. You are faced with attempting to satisfy three essential characteristics of the plan:

- the time to complete – the schedule

- the resources available – impacting the cost

- performance – the project scope and quality

Optimizing involves compressing the schedule to find an acceptable total project time consistent with resources that can be committed to the project work. As a schedule is compressed something has to give way and the first consequence is either:

- more resource capacity – everyone has to find more time for project work

- additional resources – seek additional resources.

You will attempt to use both options wherever possible.

> *Do NOT attempt to compress a schedule by just reducing duration of activities either individually or by a global percentage – no one accepts such edicts!*

When all else fails to give an acceptable result then carefully examine the estimates with the key stage owners to see if you have any scope for further reductions. The penalty you receive for compressing a schedule is normally an increase in the number and seriousness of the project risks. The initial attempts at compression must be based on finding ways to do more of the work in parallel – more concurrent activities. The schedule is like a balloon. If you hold a balloon and compress it on a horizontal axis, the diameter on the vertical axis increases as the air inside must go somewhere. This is analogous to increasing the number of parallel pathways in the plan logic diagram. If you have more pathways the risk must increase since a slippage of any pathway could affect the whole schedule.

The critical path is dynamic so any change to the logic now will probably cause this path to move to a different route through the logic diagram. If you continue to compress a balloon too much it bursts! So will your schedule, when you compress to the point where resource needs become impossible and the risks increase beyond reasonable control.

When you have compressed to the point where you can meet the expected date look for any further opportunities for concurrency. Note carefully the additional risks incurred for more concurrency, reduced durations and changes to resource needs. This information will be valuable for discussion with your sponsor and customer when they try to pressure you to reduce the schedule even further! Compression may highlight some aspects of scope and quality that you question. You may have to inform your customer that the consequences of too much compression are a reduction of quality or further constraints on the project scope. This is a subject for the final negotiation with your customer.

Using critical path analysis

If you have analysed your logic diagram, you can use some additional tricks to help the optimization process:

1. Review the relationships – if they are all *finish to start*, (ie an activity must finish before the next one starts) look at whether others will help reduce time:

- *start to start* (two activities must start together)

- *finish to finish* (two activities must finish together).

2. Split an activity into two and take the forced start of another activity from the first half of the split – known as a *lead*.

3. Utilize some of the float time available where obvious resource conflicts occur.

It is preferable not to use float time at this stage unless essential as this spare time is more useful to you during the execution of the work. Float time gives you some freedom for:

- replanning

- accommodating errors in estimating

- time to solve problems that arise.

The steps towards the optimum schedule are time-consuming but help you and your team to increase confidence. Finally you will achieve a schedule that you know is realistic and acceptable to your customer – subject to securing resource commitments from line managers. The time you spend now in optimization is a valuable investment to save time later.

> *The optimum solution is one that does not increase risks to an unacceptable level but gives a schedule you can resource and negotiate as agreed with your customer.*

Identify and secure resources

If you have optimized the schedule after completing the

resource analysis you must now identify the people available to carry out the work. The allocation of the tasks in each key stage must be agreed with the line managers for each person involved as discussed in Step 4 (Identify the Resources). With all resources identified you must use your powers of influence to get commitments from resource line managers. This is not always easy and sometimes may need the additional support of the project sponsor.

When these commitments are assured you can complete the missing data in the resource analysis tables for each key stage.

Doing it all again

You may now face the final scene of the planner's nightmare! You have optimized the schedule and find a shortage of resources has extended the schedule again. Don't act surprised, just expect this to happen. You must then return to your optimization process again and look for other ways to restore the schedule to the desired completion date. This could take several passes before a satisfactory, optimum result is obtained that satisfies both the customer and the resource line managers.

When you finally have a fully resourced schedule:

- update the Gantt Chart to show your final plan

- check the costs analysis and update if necessary to reflect the changes from optimization

- copy the resource analysis tables to the relevant resource line managers to remind them of their commitments.

Congratulations. You now have a resourced and optimized schedule that meets customer expectations – at the moment.

VALIDATION AND PLAN APPROVAL

Now that you have an acceptable plan it is tempting to dive in and start the work. Resist! There are still a few things you need to action in the planning process before launching into the project work. The sub-steps involved are shown below.

Review the risks

Have any new risks appeared as a result of planning? Look at the list of risks you recorded before planning started and ask:

- Have any risks changed to become less or more serious?

- Have you incorporated into the plan agreed actions to prevent serious risks occurring?

- Have any new risks appeared during the planning and optimization processes?

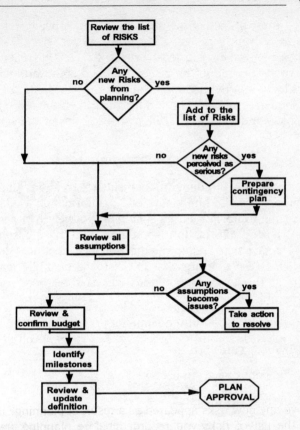

The answers will give you some more work. Previously identified and new risks agreed as serious threats to the project must be examined to prepare:

- contingency plans in case they actually occur
- triggers or signals that these risks are about to happen
- preventative action plans where possible.

If you think a risk is now unlikely to ever happen do NOT remove it from your list. Keep it on the list, since it may still pop up when you least expect it later. This ensures everyone involved in the project will be kept aware of the possibility that the risk may still occur. It is also useful for subsequent evaluation of performance when the project is complete and when asking which risks occurred and why.

Review your assumptions

It is normal and common to make assumptions during planning. You can rarely have all the information available that you would like during planning. Rather than spend time chasing information, sometimes you make assumptions to save time and noting that you'll check it out later.

Now is the time for that check to be carefully made. Examine the list of assumptions you have recorded – you did record them of course! With your team ask:

- Are all our assumptions valid?

- How many are correct?

- Which ones have not been verified?

- Can we verify the remainder now?

- Have any become *issues* that must be resolved before the launch?

- Can we set target dates for removal of outstanding issues?

- Who is going to resolve these issues?

Clearly identify the target dates when issues must be resolved to avoid a serious impact on the project schedule.

Resolving issues

If appropriate at this stage alert the sponsor and customer to the existence of such issues outstanding. Doing this now ensures the sponsor and customer understand that future serious issues (ie outside your authority to act) will be escalated for a decision to be taken.

> *An issue is a risk that has happened regardless of whether we identifed that risk.*
>
> *Issues MUST be resolved promptly to avoid schedule slippage.*

If issues escalate, you must offer some recommended actions for resolution. The sponsor may not accept your suggestions but do highlight the consequences of doing nothing eg: the effect on project costs and resourcing, on project schedule time and on quality. If issues are left unresolved they will eventually have some impact on the schedule.

PROJECT SCHEDULE
[MILESTONES AS CONTROL POINTS]

RISKS   **ISSUES**

All schedules contain a variable level of risk and it is essential that you have an understanding of the potential consequences.

When risks happen and become issues the reaction time is often critical if the schedule is to be maintained.

Control of the project work, avoiding issues requires you and your team to continually focus on identifying and anticipating all risks and promptly resolving all risks that occur and become issues.

Your future success is dependent on this control process.

All risks are predictable – except 'Acts of God'

Unfortunately our crystal ball is often cloudy preventing us seeing all the potential risks at any moment! Remind the team regularly to anticipate risks by asking:

What could go wrong at the next stage?

This may prevent surprises appearing at your project meetings.

Review and confirm the budget

Although you have updated your cost data to reflect any schedule changes resulting from the optimization process, you must now update any budget documentation prepared earlier. Verify you have collected all the cost data for the final plan and that this information is currently accurate. Enter this data into the key stage plan and derive the cumulative budget for the project. If a contingency is to be included show this separately. This will give you the *Budget At Completion*, known as the 'BAC'. This is your target cost to meet for the project work.

If there is any significant adverse variance between the BAC now derived and the original budget this becomes an issue to be resolved. Refer the issue to your sponsor for a decision. Clearly any reduction in the budget that has been derived from the plan may have a serious impact on quality or scope. Such changes will probably affect the definition as well and a dialogue with the customer will become essential.

Set the project milestones

The final action to complete the planning before seeking approval is to set the milestones in the plan. Compare the project milestone with its origins. As the word implies it was a stone marker to show some important data, miles covered and miles to go between two significant points. Similarly in the project the milestone is a significant marker in your road map – the project logic diagram.

> *The project milestone is a significant event in the project plan. It is therefore a control point and has zero duration.*

Milestones are used for measuring progress and need to be located at appropriate intervals of time, *not* many weeks apart. Often the milestone is located inside a key stage. Each milestone must identify a significant happening:

- completion of an interim deliverable

- completion of a project deliverable

- staged generation of benefits

- delivery of hardware or equipment

- any type of third party supply

- a specific review or audit point in the project

They are used for reporting progress as a measure of success. All milestones must satisfy the *SMART* test used for deliverables. (See Step 1)

Record all milestones in a simple table or schedule to

59

show planned date, forecast date and actual date achieved. This will be useful for controlling the project later and give you valuable evaluation data.

Now you are ready to seek approval of the plan from your sponsor and customer.

Approval of the plan

Collect all the plan information together and review what you have done. If you are satisfied that the plan is comprehensive and detailed enough to start the work it can be submitted to the sponsor initially for approval.

> *Do not start the project work until the customer has approved the plan*

LAUNCH THE PROJECT

Once the plan has received approval to proceed it is valuable to hold a launch meeting attended by everyone involved. There is often a dip in momentum after the intense activity of planning and you must sustain enthusiasm and focus on some key actions before launching into the work.

Preparing for launch

It is easy to encourage everyone to start work before you have clearly set out your operating ground rules. The success of the project is dependent on good communication:

- with the sponsor and customer

- with the other stakeholders

- within the project team

- with other teams working on related projects.

Communication is formal through reports of progress and informal through regular face-to-face contact. Both are essential to keep you informed of progress, problems arising and risks anticipated by the team.

Formal reporting process

Decide how you want progress to be reported and the format of these reports. Design a universal one pager to focus on:

- milestones achieved and due
- issues outstanding
- actions taken to correct slippages
- forecasts of future performance.

These reports are then used for the whole project or each key stage. Ask your key stage owners to report formally at an appropriate interval – either weekly or two-weekly. At periods of high risk have weekly reports and keep the distribution list short.

Talk to your sponsor about how issues arising are to be dealt with in this phase. Prompt action is essential to keep the project moving and avoid demotivating the team. Everyone needs to know the process you will use.

Informal reporting process

Encourage everyone to promptly tell you:

- what is happening
- what is not happening that should be happening
- when they meet roadblocks and difficulties.

Use an 'open-door' policy and always be prepared to give

support and guidance to them. Hold regular one-to-one discussions with the sponsor and each team member to talk about their work, performance and aspirations. Encourage them to give feedback and avoid surprises at project meetings.

What meetings do you need?

Draw up a schedule of essential meetings and dates in advance. Consider what you need:

- one-to-ones with the sponsor and team members
- meetings with the team (weekly/two-weekly)
- meetings with stakeholders (monthly)
- problem-solving meetings (as required)

If there is nothing to discuss cancel the meeting. Regular status meetings should be short (less than one hour) to review progress. Derive a timed standard agenda and focus everyone on expectations:

- what has not been done that should have been done
- what can be done now to correct the slippages
- outstanding issues and action plans to resolve them
- what the team anticipate could go wrong looking ahead
- a review of the work estimates for the next period
- a review of resource availability for the next period
- corrections to the plan based on results so far.

Avoid getting into involved debates and discussions by taking the issues off-line to another meeting with just the relevant people present.

Project meetings are necessary, but remember they are preventing the work itself progressing.

The launch meeting

Call together everyone who has a direct interest in the project – the sponsor, customer, team and other stakeholders to celebrate the launch. Use the meeting to get the sponsor to reinforce the importance and context strategically for the project.

- explain your plan and particularly the areas of high risk

- explain the communication processes you intend to use

- explain how you will monitor and track progress

- expose the meetings schedule and request compliance

- ensure everyone understands their role in the project.

This meeting reinforces your leadership, focuses everyone on quality and avoids a slow drift into activity when time permits. Stress the importance of personal time management so that the essential time is given to the project work.

Now finally you can say 'Let's do it' knowing you have a realistic and detailed plan to work with, that is accepted by the team and will be continually reviewed to ensure success.